At the tu
human beings ha ....
wondrous sphere. I didn't buy any of the Y2K
nonsense, but I saw tremendous effort and resource
being applied to an afterthought for the purposes of
remedying a reality none of the smartest people in the
world could foresee. Corrections were made and
compliances met, we survived entering the new
aspect of a calendar.

In the first years of the new millennium I
began writing; it was all I could do after I suffered a
back injury from a car accident. I got rear-ended
early one morning picking up sundries to get the day
started. It was shortly after the WTC attacks. Now
the smartest people in the world almost dropped the
ball on something as simple as adding an allowable
digit to an expanding numeration of days. I settled
on having the wisdom that even the smartest folks in
the world can be dumb asses and thought to myself,
How do we avoid such a thing again?

I thought of all those things I had been
exposed to growing up and it seemed to me those
who were artists were truly the smartest folks around
and for one reason. They owned creative intention.
So in the earliest days of my writing I came up with
an idea I called *The Gathering.* The function of this
gathering was to bring creative types together and
deal with mutually problematic issues humanity
faced. I am not talking about rock concerts as fund
raisers either.

In this gathering, folks of a creative nature
would share the process of being creative and teach it

0

to others wanting the wisdom offered. It was a fledgling idea, but the words made it a consideration anyways. The years that followed brought fear, hate, division and personal agendas. And in 2010 all of these flaws are the tools of manipulating populations.

In the past year I have written 10 pieces of literature covering 5 genres. All the work has been presented to the public. It has been reviewed and all are well received. Yet because of personal agenda and toleration of hypocrisy, people such as myself, who are unwilling to play the game designed by self serving people, we are not welcome into the avenues of traditional marketing sources. Getting our material in front of the readers is almost an impossibility.

Faced with the reality of writing fine material otherwise ignored, I decided to write a piece nobody ignored. Convoking Hell didn't provide the ignition I thought it would, so I present you with Hypocronance. This piece of writing that explains why we live in the world as it is, and it has everything to do with how you choose to live your life. My hope is that you'll either come to understand that you aren't as smart as you think you are, or that your wisdom is solid and you need to step up and do the right thing.

As always, I know myself to be inspired by My Creator. I am only a tool for his use in this life. We here at My Mutt Publications are creating *The Gathering* I thought about so many years ago. We seek the creativity of anyone looking to go beyond the walls of *elite* separation. Our world is changing, and all of us have more in common with each other than we have in difference. It is time to exploit that

1

thinking. The only way to do that is to know who and what it is that prohibits our tendency.

We can sit in our own little word and ignore natural truths. We can even cast a vote for hope, but until we understand the duplicities working against us, we will remain fragmented.

Take time to digest the read and become enlightened because those claiming to be expert only have the result of absolute failure. It is time for their nitwittery to be dismissed.

MH. Petry

HYPOCRONANCE

by Martin H. Petry

Hypocronance...

...is the marriage of two words. Its importance is what every bi-pedal humanoid should understand. There is no etymological description of this word, but I see a need to create convenient coining of words, just as many would see to redefining of important words used in our American Culture. Hypocrisy and Ignorance seem to be two words we bi-pedaled average humanoids endure. Some of us see things with practicality and truly know natural laws based in common sense thinking. Others of us, more than the practical minded folks, feel their way through a sort of entitled way of observation. Believing they can make Utopia. The marriage of these two words is where those of a practical nature try to explain to our significantly entitled others that Utopia is bullshit.

Because Americans find a place in our world as global leaders we have an ability to make our lives into dreams from desire of purpose. We have for the most part, peaceful living and we enjoy high quality living standards compared world wide. We are 200+ years old and we have an affinity for individual aspirations. We have given authority to governance responsible to seeing to the general welfare of a people and some say differently as to what general welfare means.

Some say the purpose of government is to provide certainty of an individual's freedom to make his/her own path through this life free from governing intrusion, while living within the laws of society. Others might say it is the purpose of the government to see to the needs of individuals that can't or won't see to their own path. As governance is authorized to see to the general welfare of its citizenry, it is also authorized to tax the wealth of our collective for doing the business of general welfare.

Just as there are two sides to a marriage there are two sides to hypocronance. This word defines how hypocritical representation and ignorant voters find themselves struggling in a de-evolutionary battle leading us to this time during late February of 2010.

The world is in financial chaos. Nations war over theological supremacy guised by economic interest prioritized for precious resource advantage, all while the benefit of our technology is consideration, tempting us to lose track of who we are because of how we arrived here.

So many of us will never know that food people ate actually came from the ground. Many of us will never know what it is like to not have running water. Science has given us the ability to escape the Grim Reaper, for a time. It has allowed us to do anything we set our focus upon and will continue to do so for our employing our wisdom.

We are a young nation, one full of promise and potential. In our youth it is easy to forget the sacrifices of our ancestors or the importance of ritualistic traditions they offered for their successes. We inherit their bounty without knowing the true cost for accumulating it. Without knowing the cost it is hard to fathom a real value for the bounty of such blessings.

I'd like to say for ease of contemplation that hypocronance should be considered as marriage of the voting public to those in representation guided by The American Constitution. With that said we must come to understand the dynamic of both.

The marriage of a man and woman allows each to act independently as part to the marriage. The pair also acts interdependently as well as dependently for the union. The legacy of the union is born of their procreation. Children are a result as one aspect by the truth to living.

Now for those of an alternative type of lifestyle choice, I recognize civil unions as partners and for understanding the dynamic of hypocronance, civil unions are = to marriage. I mention the difference because natural procreation is not a result for the alternative union and no legacy can be made for the pairing, not any legacy of procreation.

While we understand our own choice to make a life even if it doesn't include a life legacy, the dynamic for the marriage is where hypocronance dwells.

In the marriage of representative to voter there must be a conveyance and that message is conveyed by our media and free press.

Hypocrites and Ignorant beings can exist to either side of the marriage at any given time. Perception of reality, truthful by natural law arrived at for common sense thinking is paired or matched to the desire of imagining more than what reality is or can be is the point of difference within the marriage.

The manipulation of critical thinking occurs at the departure of a free press abandoning their primary purpose of being watch dogs of those elected to office.

This abandoning of a journalistic integrity for an editorial reporting serves to dumb down the crux of any national policy. Editorial reporting is commanded by talking heads who are presumably the most knowledgeable folks to lend advice. The only problem is they are all part of the nitwittery, which cherry-picks news, rather than reporting news as it should be reported.

These same broadcasters now offer the masses who tune into TV a type of reality format inclusive of audience participation baited with reward and face-time. They command the ratings of people who just don't know enough to make an informed vote about policy. The bait is a promise to value whatever those tuning into view the program need to digest for their own want not to know or care about important choices they need to make.

Hypocronance exists by the hypocrites making promises to the dopes losing themselves in their existence, while convincing the dopes they have a chance at their ultimate dreams. It is a well planned marriage of duplicity and deceit sold by phrases like *fair and balanced*. All the while more folks forget the main duty of citizenship via desires and dreams of aspiring to be individually great for no more effort than commanding a remote control.

The genius of the deception is the venue for your opinion as a contestant giving you the viewer a sense controlling your own choice for participation.

The evidence of this is very simple to see. If you work in a place with a group of people, see what the conversation of the day is during any break. The conversation likely follows any reality TV show results from the night before. Not the importance of a vote being taken in the late hours of the evening so that the result of the vote just becomes law.

You can deny what has been written above and that is what is being counted upon. They want you to feel well informed about issues of the land all while they are sure you are tuning in to Survivor or American Idol so the discussion of any social interaction is taken as omniscient wisdom.

I thought of this word back during the 2000 elections. I saw an ugliness happening in front of my very eyes when the Bush campaign victimized the McCain campaign during the primaries. Here were two candidates from the same side of the political fence slinging the vilest of utterances towards each other for the sake of dirty politics. Dirty Politics is the game and it has evolved to a new low.

Issues are no longer discussed as policy guidelines. They are discussed as barter for whoever sounds better, while surviving what is called debate. Today the moderators of debate are the ring masters of teleprompter sound bits designed for impacting audience ignorance.

I see none of the styles of debate I learned back when schools taught critical thinking skills. What I do see is more or less answers to questions the media seems to think is important. The responses are given without declarative result. So what we digest is the image of how we thought the debater appeared, as opposed to the ability to argue a postulation. The real crime of it comes down to the redefining of a once useful venue to distinguish a candidate. Now it seems that we result in the winner of a popularity contest.

Do you recall the 2004 elections and the democratic primary debates? Do you remember that at least five of the contenders spoke to decriminalizing marijuana? Now that it is 2010, has Pot been decriminalized? Those are the questions which infuriate me. They aren't questions that would allow a candidate to reveal a plan in say balancing budgets... they are soft questions used to characterize the credibility of a candidate on a social level rather than a managing job requirement.

If you don't see the point of how the media is complicit in this dynamic of Hypocronance it is likely that you never will understand the dynamic.

Even if you can't get your head around this dynamic you must have a point of view as to why you feel one way or another in our bi-cameral legislative process. None of that really matters one way or another, everyone is entitled to an opinion.

My question to you is this; on what do you base your thinking? Is it a personal issue because you are well studied on your position, or is it a group thinking type of conclusion based on listening to what the MSM tells you?

Are you assumptive about things or do you know of them first hand? The media has a purpose. Ratings are the measure that networks gauge their success by and ratings lead to profit. And profit as well as ego derived from profit decides the news presented.

I like to say today's MSM is the whore that came between the marriage of representation and constituency. Whores deplete the sanctity of marriage, so instead of a representation paying attention to its constituency, it favors the press justifying service to such as being good for the marriage. This, at face value is a contradiction.

Representation maintains the image appropriate for the media because it knows of media tactics in backlash for disregarding what the media values as worthy news. At that point representation abdicates its obligation to the constituency it was sent to serve. It does so because of something called political correctness.

It is not one side of representation or the other that falls victim to the whore's calling of need. Both are victim, the examples are endless. Better yet, apologizing for those examples has become acceptable with no real consequence for the action realized. The Gap in the marriage of representation and constituency can only be bridged by the one thing everyone wants. That is profit and a very big profit at that. If your basis of our collective reality is only from MSM can you see how Hypocronance is manifested? Media lures you to what they want to broadcast as news and worse they understand how to press your buttons.

News as once taught in journalism asked very basic questions. Those questions served the purposes of presenting newsworthy and accurate information for processing.

Who, What, When, Where, Why and How

These were the basic questions of any news broadcasting. News also validated the facts by a second or third verification of the facts as credible reporting. That is how it used to be. That is when the media or free press served the purpose of its protection under the Constitution.

Today it is quite different than its original intention. It has become more than it was ever supposed to be as an influencing agent in the stakes of candidate elections. The more one can raise funds, the more likely they can use the media to distort issues and make unrelated attributes of a competitor the losing factor. Statements that offer no qualification or disqualification to perform the task at hand become the image of what is desired rather than needed.

I do know something of what I speak to because I was educated as a marketing student at Bryant University. Image good or bad is a deciding factor among the ignorant.

The most striking example I know of for this instance is the candidacy of Mitt Romney. Mitt Romney is a self proclaimed Mormon and for his religious leaning he was labeled as a cult member, which distracted from his abundant qualifications as a leader of business. Even as Governor Mitt Romney signed into law legislation for his state, which went against his own personal values, he did so because of the job requirements.

Those who didn't know that about Mitt Romney listened to the MSM, who spoke to a potential of his cultism as a reason not to be a credible candidate as President. The presumed cultism of course went to minimize his credibility as an effective manager of bad concerns. The Salt Lake City Olympics is evidence to that ability, yet he was done in the process of primary running because people believed what the MSM wanted the ignorant to know.

You see, telling a mistruth about somebody is the easiest way to torpedo a candidacy and it was all done by those who serve the whore of media.

Another example of how the media won't report real news about someone is in the case of our President Obama.

I understood that President Obama was a follower of Black Liberation Theology before the election. I understood his thinking about the Constitution. I understood that his concern was that the Constitution didn't guarantee the authority of a federal government as he wished the document to provide. He said in his own words that he thought the Constitution needed change to ensure authority of a larger federal government.

I understood the purpose of the Constitution was written for the protection of individuals against a governing tyranny. I understood that inalienable rights men are assured of by God, not Man.

I understood that Obama was a wealth redistributionist even when the news made him out to be in favor of the middle class. His willingness to tax the highest wage earners in the land to pay for his type of governance was the evidence.

I understood then that his type of governance would lead to an increase in unemployment because he would punish profitability.

I understood President Obama as the highest ranked liberal in the senate and that his experience as an executive was woefully lacking.

Meanwhile, a Governor in the opposite camp was portrayed as being without executive experience. Her partner was the presidential candidate running as a conservative. I knew that everything in his political career demonstrated that he was anything but conservative for the legislation he wrote.

While one reality was being distorted for popularity, the other was attributed incorrectly even as the facts told otherwise.

How is this possible? Well it is possible because of the term, Hypocronance. Remember hypocrisy blended with ignorance under the manipulations of vacated journalistic integrity.

Is it not evident that the promises made by the candidate Obama have yet to be implemented as told for being elected President? Isn't that the definition of hypocrisy? Saying one thing while doing another?

Those who believed in the hypocrisy are either ignorant or just stupid. I'll give them the benefit of the doubt because we all know ignorance is curable. Judging by the polling data today the axiom to the curability of being ignorant is still valid.

What is also valid is the notion that Hypocronance will not reveal its own truth. Electing Obama didn't result in his promises of campaigning, all while the economy worsens the media continues to favor him for as long as they can. They will not own up to their disingenuous methodology for selling an incompetent candidate.

Chris Mathews is a guy who is guilty of that and by his own words. As a so called journalist he said, "I am willing to do whatever it takes to make this thing a success."

That was regarding the election of Obama to the presidency. And for the election to the presidency he was successful, but he tied his journalistic credibility to the success of Obama and he still has a job. Why?

Well because of the ignorant folks who think he is a journalist rather than an editorialist, allow for such incompetence without facing consequence.

Chris Mathews never faced accountability for those comments. If he did face the consequence of his action, why isn't he seeing to facilitating a remedy to the failure of his offering?

There are few public figures that follow the guidelines of respectable reporting of news. Those who don't report the information respectfully conceive Utopia at that moment. They are fully convinced that their doing is a benefit by an example through ill conceived thinking and poor leadership.

Leadership is a funny thing, in terms of leading a people. Leadership for attaining the presidency cost Obama $650 million. That means a vote is worth $2.25. Obama solicited $5 donations from emailing they did during the candidacy and he got a great return for doing so.

Obama represented those wanting and believing in Utopia, or at least a fairness of a perceived injustice and they bought Obama's pretense of leading the country into the Promised Land. In doing, so the progressive philosophy of politics owned the executive branch and picked up seats on a majority from both houses of congress. The Grand Illusion of better days had arrived.

I know a thing or two about leadership. I've been a leader my whole life. When President Obama was elected, I knew it wouldn't be long before the surge of ignorant chaos that swept him into the office would soon ebb. I even made mention that the same surge would crush him for his lack of leadership as I knew what leadership meant.

Hypocronance creates a reality in which truth of leadership becomes exposed for what it is. That happens because the Utopia promised is never a natural truth and can never become a proper reality as a result of poor leadership. As of this writing a year has passed since Obama became President.

All his foreign visits it has been for no gain of American Interest. Yesterday he held a summit on Healthcare of a bi-partisan nature. His intention was to pass anything that could come from his reform of nationalized Healthcare before the coming mid term elections.

2/26/2010 11:51 a.m.

I made that notation because President Obama spoke to having a decision of the bill within three to six weeks. One way or another, he expected healthcare reform to be done with by whatever means its completion would be required. He has at his disposal a congress of his party's majority and they may pull the trigger on a reconciliation vote, only requiring 51 votes to pass the bill.

It is my thinking that he will push for the reconciliation vote and try to push through the bill. If he can't manage passing the bill for the 51 vote majority then his leadership is a failure. Now I could be wrong and if I am then I'll stand corrected.

But when it becomes apparent that support for this bill can't muster a majority rather than the 51 votes needed for reconciliation, Hypocronance will be validated on the back of leadership.

Last night while watching the summit on healthcare the media couldn't help itself by having cut out reports of those watching as well, in this case it was worthwhile. A self-proclaimed democrat who characterized himself as a pro-choice voter said, "We should vote for the conservatives because they just do it better."

He capitulated on his folly of Hypocronance. The comment for hearing it struck me as being a final blow to the constraints of ignorance. He witnessed the limits of arrogance crumble under the pressures of natural law. He has been enlightened.

I wrote a piece called *The Gathering* many years ago. It may have been while the word Hypocronance came to my thinking and thusly, my coining of the word.

My editor is gonna kill me...

The Gathering is an attempt to unify reasonable thinkers. I'm also of mind to use it for the gain of people who are interested in reasonable thinking.

The work to follow is but one of many topics to be analyzed, deliberated, and debated. It is the hope that we as the people of the world may in fact, enlighten ourselves to better living.

One thing is for sure... things could be better. Enlightenment is a process.

Consider how you may have become enlightened about anything... Usually it happened through realization of things pertaining to you. Rarely does it occur instantaneously. As this work is meant to benefit many, a consensus must be arrived at. Hence, *The Gathering*.

The world is seemingly in a reactionary period. We as a people seem to be burdened by issues, rather than management of them. Fire-fighting is a term widely recognized in dealing with crisis. Reasonable thinking may avert what is a seemingly dark future. Reasonable thinking is not reasonable because it is claimed to be reasonable. It is reasonable because hard truths are discussed, followed by an effort to respond to them as opposed to react towards those truths.

The first part of *The Gathering* will be shared in the following pages. We shall discuss Power and attributes of it, as well as misconceptions to it. Many other ideas will be reasonably thought out in future assemblages of *The Gathering*.

Martin H. Petry

Power...
The ability or capacity to act or perform effectively...
One definition from The American Heritage Dictionary. Suitable for our purposes.

In The United States of America, we have an extraordinary amount of power. Yet in our world, there is much ill will towards us. There are several valid reasons for this.

As we are facing some difficult times as a people, it is reasonable to assume that we don't have an efficient power base, powerful yes but not effective. If it were, the future wouldn't be so bleak or dark.

So we begin.
In our consideration of power, we should think of power as a triangle. Power Triangle.

The three sides will be; leadership, integrity and motivation.

Positions of power exclusive to government will also be discussed. We shall then note a difference. Politicians and Public Servants. Reasonable thinking will favor Public Servants. Politicians, well they will be considered with scrutiny, and by example in The Gathering.
Let us move forward with discussions of leadership, and its place in the power triangle.

There is exceptional leadership where those follow en masse. There is satisfactory leadership where those follow because it is a means to an end. There is less than satisfactory leadership when power struggles and chaos abounds.

Leadership is a rare quality. Excellent Leaders are rarer indeed. In the definition of power, leadership might have an association towards ability to perform. Some will tell you leaders can be taught... that might be true, however, teaching excellence is truly difficult. Most teachers aren't excellent.

That is part of a piece I wrote in the early days of the new millennium, within two years of the new millennium.

There is a flow to that writing which supports a notion of power related in the definition of leadership. In thinking about Hypocronance, power is also tied to Hypocronance at the hip. The dynamics of Hypocronance touch natural laws as well as perceived realities. All while leadership and power remain points on a compass leading to a destination.

It is worth mentioning that while leadership comes from the ability of an individual to lead it must be regarded as unique to the individual. Power on the other hand, is not unique to the individual unless the authority of power is bestowed to the leader of selection.

In President Obama's case a less than satisfactory leadership would be applied for the evidence at hand. The media in this case isn't doing the job of its original authority under the guise of journalistic integrity. Rather it promotes the result of poor leadership, all while it controls a profit flow based upon ratings.

The economy is in shambles with unemployment taking a back seat, which makes no sense at all when pondering leadership. The President is trying to manipulate laws for a benefit unfunded, while the country endures an economic stall. It might be in better interest for President Obama to secure the vitality of a productive populace, which pays taxes and also pays premiums for the discussed benefit of health. Yet unemployment is likely to expand while requiring businesses to absorb costs the government really has no authority to impose.

An excellent leader would have never entertained such a discussion. A satisfactory leader might not ever have needed the discussion, certainly one such as yesterday.

The authority of ignorance grants power. It grants power that is weak at heart and is fickle. Those who live by the heart's desire and grant authority to ineffective leadership which never delivers the desire of intention will always be the chaos demanding what they bought into. That is the folly of their dynamic within Hypocronance.

When those weak at heart realize the betrayal as perceived the power granting the authority becomes unfriendly, impatient and downright disagreeable.

The media that promotes the fraud turns against the thing it profited for in supporting and ultimately scavenges the remains of its own forced betrayal to the unsatisfactory leadership.

I believe that to be the reality of the current President. Even though Hypocronance may abound supporting ineffective leadership, natural law will demand that poor leadership face a consequence. The consequence is profitability, or in the name of Presidential Leadership an ability to have revenue stream from a vibrant economy to fund such laws.

Here is a law those blinded in Hypocronance will never accept. Effective leadership skills aren't something that can be taught. Effective leadership is born to individuals. President Obama has been educated by a system that believed in a Utopia where such things as leadership were thought to be teachable. In fact President Obama had one of the finest educations this land could provide. Hypocronance as a dynamic demanded its fair share for the Utopia desired. At the altar of leadership the progressive tendency of Obama's leadership has unraveled. Chaos ensues and the world is waiting on result. People depending on leadership aren't convinced that the decision of authorizing said leadership is a place they can remain.

Effective leaders have the ability to convince others to do something they might not want to do as being a course of action, which will insure a better destination for the journey.

Progressive leadership can't convince those who see to the effectiveness of any design, or why it is best to follow them into a reality that holds no promise of anything more than expanded chaos. That is the dynamic of Hypocronance manifested in today's leadership of our nation. Our majority of government leadership can not come together in agreement that our healthcare should be fixed. They all sit in similar agreement that the problem at hand needs some type of better management. Until the chaos is dismissed nobody espouses a path to better management of the problem without the help of the whore that is media.

Hypocronance is a condition of human folly and some are more susceptible to the folly of it than others. The truth of Hypocronance lies in the want for something, which without sound leadership can never be achieved.

Take for instance, healthcare... Hypocronance lives in the fraud of addressing the healthcare concern in America. The ignorant don't really see or know how more than tort reform, interstate purchase options and denial of benefits to illegal aliens would help the problem.

They are accurate in that addressing those issues would be helpful. The problem is what insurance companies will never tell you.

Insurance companies make money by collecting premiums; they don't make money paying claims. If a patient is going to die, they'd rather have the death occur before long term benefits would have to be paid.

The first issue to be considered within a philosophical context would be the social acceptance of mortality. Are people accepting that life ends? Are they intending to prolong the life experience of their own condition beyond a sensible acceptance to their mortality?

The second issue to consider is that there is a cost associated to prolonging a life experience. In the 80's there was a similar conversation and it was called HMO legislation. During that time government designed regulations of the medical industry prompted by insurance companies interested in profiting under Health Maintenance Organizations.

The result is that which we face now. You see, the same people who negotiate deals as they exist based upon the law of large numbers, are the folks being regulated by the government.

Now these people are special, they are like the man behind the green curtain. They don't really mention to you while negotiating your benefit that they already know what their profit margin is for the explanation.

You see these folks take your money then they tell doctors and health institutions what they are going to pay for regarding their insured group.

The HMO laws from the 80's are the primary issue of our problems today. They remain a monopoly and the ignorant see cures of the problem as tort reform, interstate purchases along with paying illegal alien benefits as direct results for operating as a monopolized business. The regulatory agency within the government also deals with a government operated insurance agency as well. Two entities exist and a third if you see insurance expansion to social security. Both the insurance companies and the government create the conditions, which allow for a need of curative remedies, but they don't simplify the problem. They act as agencies between a doctor and his/her patient. They dictate what the costs are and how business is done. All while nobody has given a value to what any limit of care might just be based upon any acceptance of cost associated to mortality.

Now the real issue behind healthcare is this: it must be paid for and the crisis of healthcare is being based on cost analysis when the economy that pays for the premiums is at a complete stall.

When you see further into the future you have to account for the demographic of those who used to contribute to the system, known as baby boomers. They will become non-contributors as being retired. The earning potential of these people represent huge loss of revenue to the government who will be overseeing premiums for said healthcare. If you don't know the cost, how do you pay for the program?

For those who live in the folly of Hypocronance, healthcare is a perceived entitlement. They think that health insurance is a right. The truth of it is very different. Rights of men under the authority of the Constitution, which are inalienable aren't granted by men to men, they are granted by God as the founders understood the infinity of a higher power.

In a time like today, when hypocrites convince the masses that we can accomplish anything, even against what natural law dictates; we face the difference of personal responsibility to a condition, rather than guarantee to a condition, never promised as a right.

The inability to overcome natural law for the arrogance of Hypocronance makes the reasoned and practical thinker an enemy to the masses. What ensues is stalemate. Ultimately anger results because the assumption of what is a right is revealed as nothing more than a personal choice. The insidious nature of Hypocronance dictates entitlement or the sense of entitlement as the expected result, well before the discussion of rights is ever spoken.

For instance: Are children under the age of majority entitled to rights as citizens or not?
Depending on what your conclusion is for the question illustrates whether you are of a practical mind, or a mind of your heart's desire.

Is it important to maintain a culture of diversity or abide nationalized acceptance of American culture?

Societies thinking of such questions offer an invitation allowing Hypocronance to flourish. That ultimately leads us to chaos, because those wanting Utopia can not place an acceptable value to fund Utopia.

Without knowing such a value there can be no solution to the problem. But because those entitled believe that it is impossible to not overcome natural law, the undefined problem assumes the nature of desperation needing to solve the crisis, yet the obvious solution, even when presented is discarded as being immoral.

Morality is another word which is consistently misused by those in the folly of Hypocronance.

Moral: relating to, dealing with, or capable of making the distinction between right or wrong in conduct.

That is the Webster's New World College Dictionary Fourth edition first definition of *moral* as stated. If you read the words defining a moral you'll see that a moral is singular by subject. Meaning the moral for one man, may not be what is considered moral for another. The manner in which society dictates rules as to wrong or right for the collective is known as *mores*.

Mores: folkways that are considered conducive to the welfare of society and so, through general observance, develop the force of law, often becoming part of a formal legal code.

The same dictionary used to provide the above definition is the reference.

So, one man's morality isn't the issue. Who is to say what the character of any individual is, when they act within the parameters of societal mores? If law in force doesn't require action from a formed legal code, why do those in the folly of Hypocronance always make the claim that unwillingness to embrace Utopia as they believe Utopia to be, demonstrates a lack of morality? It must be incumbent of those living in chaos within the folly of hypocronance to make their Utopia a reality settled upon legal code of forced law to include such a complaint. Otherwise it becomes a tactic of diversion, employed by passive aggression ignoring the uniformity of the society based upon a definition of a word in which they fail to parse correctly.

If there is one institution which has done more than any other to embrace the mediocrity of Hypocronance, it is the media. The freshest example I can think of, occurred today.

I watched a New York news telecast this morning from one of the local networks. This morning much of the Northeast part of the country which has endured several winter storms with high yields of frozen precipitation. A news report spoke of an Interstate Highway closing along the New York border with Connecticut.

The report indicated that there were hundreds of cars stranded on a forty mile stretch of road. Children with parents in cars had been stranded up to fourteen hours. Media being what it is, took the opportunity to remind local emergency respondents that enough wasn't being done for the children's sake. The two reporting nitwits were asking for certainty requiring more than professionalism was attending.

The example of media dictating its morality based upon a Utopia, gave voice to all of those watching the report living in the folly of Hypocronance an invitation to demand that such an injustice as folks being stranded was unacceptable, especially while children are involved.

I would have liked to have a word with those reporters demanding Utopian response based upon their desired morality from the state's infrastructural maintenance authority while reporting the reality of the condition.

In the moments and hours of a climatic condition, which interrupted human life, at least one media concern looked to do other than report the news. A phone call made from one of the so-called stranded drivers was the credibility of their reporting, rather than the system seeing to the crisis reported. Any practical minded people listing to the report might have known that driving in a blizzard would likely result in a prohibition to travel, if not result in an accident. They would say, those are the risks of winter driving in New England.

Yet there is an audience who hears the report and considers the condition unacceptable for hearing it, because such a tragedy would never exist in Utopia.

The more the media figures out the complex simplicity of those watching, the more they employ the technique of making the news a national priority. They will distort conditions hoping the folks who are good hearted but ignorant of practical realities keep watching as the tragic occurrence is a priority.

Is there not a weather service available so as to make a decision for avoiding travel in such bad weather? Are these drivers (non professional) victims of their own folly? A professional driver can use such a time as off duty on their DOT logs.

The thinking as far as I can fathom seems to try to excuse stupid people from the consequences of their own actions. That is where the folly of Hypocronance is the strongest.

Another example was a report of parents of students working in Haiti, where the aftermath of an earthquake was the crisis of the week. As bad as it is for a parent to lose a child for any reason, these people couldn't believe that our government wasn't doing everything it could do to address the crisis while considering six young girls as the priority of the crisis.

The media invited a plea from parents desperate in facing a very difficult reality. The media gave them a voice full well knowing that the desperation of their subject couldn't possibly change the reality as it unfolded through human tragedy dictated by living in a natural disaster.

The stories were cherry-picked to exploit those driven by a desire for Utopia perceived, while facing the horror of a practical reality. The media reporting of the tragedy summoned $300 million given in aide to those so desperately affected by a risk of living. That is the motive of the media, plain and simple.

The $300 million donated to those living or surviving in Haiti and many more millions were made for covering every facet they could report, which offended their sense of the unacceptable. After three weeks one or two of those daughters were found dead during the recovery phase of the disaster.

There was no voice allowed to those people then for the discovery of death. What would such reporting reveal? Certainly nothing which Utopia cannot admit? And the folly of Hypocronance moves from tragedy to ineptitude, always pointing to Utopia's meeting face to face with the practicality of natural law demonstrating chaos. All when so many believe chaos shouldn't be allowed.

To understand the pervasive nature of Hypocronance, you almost have to ponder the dynamic as being a part of any human gathering. Remember, Hypocronance is the folly of folks who believe they know better because they live life led by their heart's strings. So as you can imagine, any part of ritual in any institution falls victim to the folly of Hypocronance.

The other need of Hypocronance has to include a common wealth. This wealth has to be paid by the masses. That is so there is an open forum for the treasure of the donation or taxation. That forum is the discussion of what direction the group moves toward. Religion and Education are two gatherings of human intention that always exist in the folly of Hypocronance.

Religion or the belief in religion is a curiosity of mine. The rituals of dogma always seem to require rules and laws that I just don't comprehend. There was a time in my life when I could do nothing more than read Scripture and other religious documents.

These times were well before I thought to coin the word Hypocronance. It was the foundation that allowed for critical thinking of ritualistic mannerisms within differing dogmas that I came to be a participant of ceremony. A lot of this time has been written of in a book I co-authored with Tracy LeCates, called *Convoking Hell*. During those days I cleaved myself from authority I had no use for acknowledging.

I found my gravity pulling to the wisdom contained in the New Testament. I studied the words of Christ and began to know him as a man and part of the trinity of the Holy Ghost. Now you may think that I am a Christian because of that gravitation, but you'd be wrong. I call myself a spiritualist and I do so because within the many of folks claiming to be Christian, I have seen so many examples of those living in the folly of Hypocronance.

Christ responded directly to a question in which he was asked by a follower about how to pray. Christ responded by illustration of praying in a closet. In other scriptures Christ told many that the kingdom of heaven lies within your heart. He also said that his church would be built upon a stone where and when three gathered in thinking of his teachings.

These are simple and basic instructions from a man who did things 2,000+ years ago and somehow or another man has forgotten what Christ was teaching. They did reinvent ritual so as to guide folks to tithe abundant fortunes for creating ridiculous houses of pretense known as churches.

Now I won't condemn anyone for their faith, as long as that faith doesn't want to kill me. That being said, I could care less what your religious faith might be.

For the most part actions speak louder than worship does. We can't neglect that people with named faiths do some very holy service in the name of their faith.

It isn't my intention to condemn any of those sacrifices people make within their own wisdom of faith.

But here is the thing... within differing faiths there is an intolerance of alternative faiths. A predisposed thinking of righteousness within any faith by comparison to another is the largest reason to put pride forth before a faith. And if you are a student of the Great Teacher, he mentioned where pride would lead you.

During the writing of the Constitution, the founders thought of individual liberty while coming from places where the leaders of men dictated religious following. In those lands wars killed many for personal faith. So here in the New World, the founders craftily wrote the First Amendment, which made mention to those in power as to not make any law that would support one religion over another.

Their intent was to proclaim that any citizen had a right to worship as he saw fit for his life. Today, Hypocronance suggests that there is a separation between church and state.

The separation between church and state is a ridiculous notion, because within the founders' notes there are many thoughts suggesting that while the writing of the original documents occurred the authors had divine visitations. That is fact. There was no conclusion of separation of church and state, just impossibility for the state to endorse any one religion.

This is an important difference for many in the folly of Hypocronance. Just as there are folks who do have faith, there are others who don't have faith. More importantly to these people without faith anyone who does have faith are subjects for passive aggressive attacks for the belief.

As we see now, Christianity is under attack by those who think there is no room for God in government. The hypocritical nature of these people only seems to attack the Christian believers as they are the enemy of agnostic and atheist philosophy, especially those Christians with a tendency to be from the right.

Bills being written today of considered legislation want "In God We Trust" stricken from all forms of government issued currency as well as an end to prayer in school.

The folly of this Hypocronance is probably the most controversial of our culture. These folks are typically educated types and for being educated it is almost impossible for them to realize that human capability cannot overcome natural law. Here is why: For all the science that they study, for all the earnings made for taking risk. They have authority based upon education, which may in fact have known not a lick of experiential wisdom. They are known as the *elite*. The real problem is that because they are educated, they command a higher rate of compensation for their particular expertise.

These are folks who tend to be progressive. They welcome diversity of our nation, rather than having a unique American Culture. The other thing they realize is that unlike other average Americans, their notions of Utopia aren't well received by the silent majority. They will use courts to make legislation rather than employ the legislative body responsible for that duty. So as you would see *elites* for observation; are educated people who would like to define the First Amendment as a notion of separation of church and state for convenience of undoing the fact that this country is built upon a Judeo-Christian thought process.

They can't get support by representation for their thinking in the normal business of legislation, so they use their wealth to hire lawyers employed in arguing the constitutionality of a concern. They seek judgment from a court to enact laws they want. The examples of this are very recent and they come to us by the MA SJC in writing law allowing for GAY marriage. Hypocronance does manipulate our system and it does so through bribery and extortion from a greater ability to earn funds from their singular expert abilities.

Lawyers argue a case in front of the like-minded officials on a bench to re-write law, rather than interpret the law. These people who believe in heart's strings thinking have violated the First Amendment rights regarding religion. Then usurp a process of forming legal code by the body responsible for the enacting of legislation desired by the constituency.

Hypocronance can't be demonstrated more effectively than by those who are the progressives within our land. They utilize Hypocronance as a methodology to claim Utopia as real and attainable because they think they can. It doesn't stop in religion or political representation, either.

Those who are educated and living in the folly of Hypocronance control the world of academia. I have witnessed this personally as I was likely one of many who graduated during a time when education did in fact teach the skills necessary for providing students the skills needed to be independent in this world.

That year was 1982 and after 1985 I believe that educators through the evolution of teacher unions and Hypocronance manipulated the curriculums of public school students with a progressive type of educating process.

Along with the ACLU the NEA changed learning to include bi-lingual studies, removing certain aspects of a day that students like me knew as normal. The Pledge of Allegiance is no longer said as part of the students' day. Civic Education or the study of governance of our Constitutional Government is all but gone. Grading no longer measures a student's progress because giving measure to students for their effort is now seen as bad for the self esteem of kids.

The teacher unions have sent professional negotiators to local school districts, insuring that tenure of a teacher once attained exempted them from being fired, thereby removing the ability for superintendents and principals of schools to fire teachers who weren't serving the interests of the public as educators.

More than that, these nitwits in Academia somehow think educating children to be tolerant of homosexual awareness is acceptable. Their trump card for facing criticism of their miserable results of unsatisfactory education goes back to the parental aspect of education. Their complaint in defense of criticism of their own ineffectiveness falls to a lack of support from parents, who are otherwise busy working for two incomes to pay for the increasing cost associated to living in better places.

Tax payers who sit on school committees aren't professional negotiators and are overwhelmed by the contracts they face. And there is one more aspect worth talking about concerning the formative years of education.

That is the fact that most youngsters educated are typically educated by a teaching body only complimented by 15% male teacher ratio on average. Essentially what then happens is a natural law, which can't be argued. Little boys become older and more energetic, which results in women who teach, throwing their hands up while realizing they are unable to control these young boys. Next order of business….. Doping the kids up.

In a trust such as teaching our children how to be independent, we have those within the industry of teaching who are fostering Utopia; not the practical tools needed for the independent students we want and expect.

If you think this is nonsense, that is fine, but here is something else you will never hear. Academia doesn't only exist in the secondary schooling under the authority of public trust. Students indoctrinated for the expectation of Utopia are fulfilling the profit potential to higher learning industries for the production of mood altering chemicals prescribed for ADHD. Who creates the new drugs used to make students able to believe in this Utopia? The answer is medical colleges.

I made the mention of the date I graduated from high school because when I tried to help my daughter with her lessons at home, the material she was acclimated to learn was nothing I ever remembered for learning as a student.

Back in the day before widely accepted prescribing of drugs, my father had a solution for ADHD. That solution was in building a rock wall on our family property. That rock wall took many years to complete and any time I was too fidgety to sit and learn, my father's foot was in my ass. I humped rocks twice my body weight along with my brother to beautify the family property.

There is another dynamic which allows for public education to be the failure it is and that dynamic needs discussion. As I mentioned earlier, teachers utilize a defense for the lack of parental influence regarding education. As that is a reality there is also a more sinister reality of the parental neglect towards education. This is typically how it happens. As we all know, school time antics of children always test authority. When students go beyond the acceptable behavior of being involved in the morality of school, there are parents who will do anything and everything to insulate their nitwit children from the consequences of their own actions. They will do so by threatening a lawsuit against the school committee for adjudicating improper actions of the same students. The result of such action is a complete disaster in terms of applying discipline needed in learning for students.

In Utopia each student isn't an individual, but rather a little being that comes to school without any issues and always studies diligently. Conforming to class rules is the Utopia demanded by this folly of Hypocronance controlled by academicians.

Discipline must be taught for overcoming methods to learn difficult subject matter based by different student affinities. Some students need to buckle down and find a manner to get through material they'd rather not know. Once the threshold of bad behavior is breached, discipline of students must be an authority of those responsible for the lessons. Otherwise chaos remains the lesson.

Parents who also live within a folly of Hypocronance can't accept that their little Johnny or Jane are disruptive punks who brazenly disrupt the process of learning in actions, which become more and more dangerous to the public they are involved with as students.

Evidence of this is abundant. In the past 20 years have we seen the escalation of deviants come to school with guns in murderous actions against the school public. The claim after the fact is always by the parents, "We didn't know that little Johnny or Jane had such problems, they always seemed to be decent kids." But the response doesn't explain the reason for the example. School kids are dead, teachers are dead and the ultimate wraps of hypocrisy come to the light of day.

While the media exploits the tragedy for the folly of Hypocronance everyone involved in making the reality a tragedy points fingers at an ambiguous blaming of their own designs. This is the evolution of Hypocronance in its best demonstration.

Those wanting to live in a Utopia will not or can not face the natural laws that apply. The dynamic of wanting and buying into Utopia relieves anyone from analyzing their own actions as part of a problem; in fact the reality that demands the impossibility of Utopia creates a discussion as to what must be done to avoid such a disastrous reality ever again.

Those responsible for creating the environment become ensconced in reinventing plausible cures that only make the original problem larger than it ever began as, always with a certainty that the remedy costs more than the system can sustain.

Instead of assuming a responsibility for the tragedy, responsibility and the accepting of that responsibility seems to evaporate. Once again, when consequence for action is dismantled, what is learned? How do you solve problems if you don't know what makes the problem? If a departure from a system which worked years ago is not seen as part of the cause to current problems, where does one begin to achieve former results while remaining in the denial of responsibility?

Could it be that the new manner in teaching since 1985 is the problem? Is allowing bi-lingual study and political correctness along with tolerance of alternative living a worthy substitute for a departed rigorous curriculum of reading, writing, and 'rithmatic? What is our measure of producing competitive students worldwide? The last measure I took notice of put American students 30th on the list of achievement.

Are those in education elsewhere at higher levels than us using an indoctrination of Utopia, or are they teaching the nuts and bolts of tools needed for independent beings armed with the best possible education available?

You see, in the folly of Hypocronance excuses are given at the result of failings. Not enough money is being applied. Parents aren't doing their jobs. The requirements of diverse study of a bi-lingual nature need more resources and all at a time when those in control are thinking that wealth redistribution is a mandate of the people to invent Utopia.

Those in the folly of Hypocronance can't get away from the simple fact of natural law, even when it applies to the efforts of men. There is only a certain amount of resource available to any institution's viability. The past thinking suggests that nobody in the managerial positions of these institutions understands that simple reality. Nobody can afford the chaos of Utopia!

Sure, it would be great to think that all our kids are beyond reproach. Sure, it would be great to think that no matter what an individual's capabilities are, everyone should be considered equal. Sure, it would be nice to believe in a life that was void of competition and that just because you show up, you are granted the certification of being adult. Even though your intelligence quotient comes from a shallow pool of smarts. Sure, it would be nice to think that differing characteristics of people would be ignored, unless of course you are one who has a special need. Why, then your special need is prioritized because in Utopia you'd have to get beyond the expectations of reality ignored.

Hypocronance demands that injustices in life be dismissed. It pretends that competition is unfair and needs remedy. Hypocronance in its dynamic insulates people from realizing their own contribution to a failing of Utopia, when Utopia is the mindset of the folly. Those in the folly of hypocronance must maintain a definition of equality as something more than it was ever meant to be.

Our Constitution makes it certain that every person has an opportunity to live freely, pursuing happiness within the acceptable behaviors in our country. It doesn't guarantee that everyone is equal. But those wanting Utopia expect that equality is the reality, when nature says otherwise.

The folly of Hypocronance has strongholds in every important institution in our culture. The systemic departure from rewarding an individual for personal efforts has become taboo.

The folly of Hypocronance demands by a progressive definition that we must abide fairness in all we do. Those in the folly of Hypocronance will not yield to a time tested adage that *Life is not Fair.* Rather it is the mission of those demanding Utopia that plain observances of life as unfair should be deleted from reality.

Delusion of truth is the plague of this folly. The abundance of this delusion is now pandemic, because the truth of any matter is as simple as realizing that the truth isn't always a happy ending.

In the folly of Hypocronance, definitions are changed for convenience of some standards holding traditional meaning. The convenience of the change is rarely more than convincing the ignorant that changes of definition are in their own best interests. We have already discussed how semantics have changed the thinking of the Constitution or the interpretation of the document. But so much more has been artfully redefined for the sake of wanting a Utopia.

It is important for me to state unequivocally that I don't care about other folks' decisions of living as long as they don't prohibit or make my freedoms difficult in keeping.

That is to say I neither support nor deny choices of a personal nature. Homosexuals are a contingent of folks who have an interesting case to be made with regards to discrimination.

Upon the founding of this country, the organizing body saw fit to name marriage as a building influence, because married folks were more likely to develop a family who would be the employees needed to overcome the demands of forging a new nation.

At the time the incentive was given for the purpose of populating our country so we could embrace our liberty and pursuit of happiness. As time changed and the need to procreate diminished, laws holding to marriage as a benefit for all things exclusive to marriage became unjust in a new world. Those seeking their own personal happiness for their own choice as living became the pairings of folks and partnerships of those in an alternative lifestyle didn't have the claim to tax benefits or health permissions or benefits known to those who were married as husband and wife.

Times changed and inequity fell upon those not named in a traditional marriage. For the practical minded individual a simple resolution would have been to rewrite laws ensuring that alternative lifestyle partnerships would in fact share the same benefit of being married. Some even spoke to *civil unions*. And that by itself seemed a feasible solution for the inequity.

The folly of Hypocronance demanded that such a solution be disregarded. In fact the issues of inequity were no longer the motivation for those seeking Utopia. Those seeking Utopia made the equity issue of partnership an impossible reality in the face of natural law. The impossibility of this decision seeking Utopia came to forefront in redefining marriage as a traditional term. Now it was meant to be inclusive of the alternative, when no logic of words or understanding of word had any plausibility. The folly of Hypocronance rose to a personal resentment perceived as injustice by those wanting an alternative lifestyle in Utopian redefining.

All kinds of clichés became the buzz and once again the media focused on exploiting the condition by raising the vitriol of those damaged for the impossibility of natural law. Coming out of the Closet was just one of many phrases these folks utilized in drawing a focus upon their demand for a perceived Utopia.

Gay Pride parades became the paralysis of localities for issuances of parade permits. Ultimately the fatality of this Utopia emerged by a hapless fool elected as President of our country named George W. Bush.

Upon the insanity demanding that fags were suffering human rights violations President Bush probably uttered the most concise suggestion of his terms as President. His suggestion was simply, "Take the question of gay marriage to a Constitutional Amendment."

It is difficult for me to offer the man much of any blessings for his service. He is a nitwit who couldn't formulate a sentence in his public addresses, but on hearing that suggestion I became elated.

The measure of what is acceptable for our people has always needed the affirmation of a super majority if it was to become law of the land. The only trouble with his suggestion for the homosexual community was a stark reality that the majority of this country wouldn't tolerate the notion of same sex marriage.

For the suggestion those living in the folly of Hypocronance went crazy, because they faced the natural truth of their reality. You see same sex marriage isn't a human rights argument. It is an equitable argument for the sake of partnership.

Non acceptance of same sex marriage as law doesn't rise to the violation of inalienable rights as stated within our Constitution. Those in the minority of this thinking couldn't accept that the majority of Americans don't approve of sharing the word marriage. Civil Unions would have likely worked. For those civil unions partners would have enjoyed the same benefit of married men and women without the sameness of the name.

This goes back to the thinking within those known as *elites* unwilling to tolerate faith of another as a guiding focus within their own lives.

Marriage is traditionally a ritual of any religious dogma. It was a reality well before governments decided to license the partnership. This folly of Hypocronance lives in removing an individual's faith for the sake of fairness without competition or even character difference. The posturing of such insanity knows only intolerance of those not interested in progressivism.

Those who posture the insanity are a minority in our culture. The folly of Hypocronance gives this minority a majority within the bodies of our representation because of the ignorant, who assume to be more than their heart's strings desires, while avoiding logical process of reason.

Since the mid terms of 2006 the hijacked democrat party by progressives decided that for equality of a people it would be a good idea to put the American Tax payer on the hook for those who could have never afforded owning their own homes. The reality of living without home ownership was an anathema to the progressives seeking Utopia.

Once they took the majority, Chris Dodd, Jack Reed, Charlie Schumer and Barney Frank strong-armed lending institutions to write loans the banks would have never considered writing otherwise. Since the Clinton revisions of the 90's, deregulation of financial oversight gave insurance companies permission to sell mortgages. Previously non-allowed cross business was the way of the day. Derivatives were the new profit makers and all of these newly realized business practices were built upon mortgages and the repayment of them. During the Bush years nobody did anything to see the danger coming from doing business that way, even though the first six years of Bush denied the Community Housing Act signed by Clinton.

I don't think it was a hundred days after the government backed mortgages went into default and a couple of days after that the dominos began to fall. Shearson Lehman was the first giant of finance to signal trouble and after that, well here we are.

Unemployment is the highest since the days of the Great Depression, capital is frozen, growth is stalled and the same nitwits for our condition want to hijack one sixth of our economy by regulating healthcare. This is why I call it nitwittery.

The priority of nationalizing healthcare can't come while our unemployment rate is as high as 20+%. Revenues the government receives come from employment tax. Yet what we have is a priority of assuming a higher deficit for a notion a minority holds as being fair rather than what a diligent policy regarding getting the country back to work would demand. Talk about putting the cart before the horse.

Moreover, there is thinking a second bailout will be needed. All the while, the media speaks to those in the Tea Party Movement as being clueless for motivation. The *elites* say the tea party folks are unpatriotic all while they engage in exercising their First Amendment guarantee. Amidst the folly of Hypocronance, a CHAOS results; those who want Utopia can't figure out that profit or gain for an individual's labor is not theirs to tax without limit. To beat all of that, there is thinking that the top wage earners should pay their fair share.

They demand that as the measure of Utopia, when the inarguable reality suggests that 40% of people pay 96% of the tax burden. They dismiss the fact that making of more money puts you into a higher taxable bracket just as the system is designed.

While the Utopia "Yes We Can" notion is what those of heart's strings motivation demanded, the reality exists with unwillingness for private investors to risk anything.

In the early days of the Obama Presidency, I warned folks that his failure was inexorably linked to his inability to get lenders on board. Lenders aren't lending, those who were the risk takers aren't taking risks and our government wants to bureaucratize a health system that 85% of the people it serves are happy with, even if they think the cost associated needs some type of control.

If by now you can't get a grasp on what Hypocronance demonstrates, then I reckon you never will. I can turn on the TV and listen to a report of Hypocronance on any given day and at many different times.

Just recently, another tragedy took place in Busch Gardens, Florida at SeaWorld. A forty year old whale trainer was killed by a Killer Whale while working off stage with the whale. In as much as it sucks that this woman died for one reason or another - and I say that because the actual footage of the incident hasn't been revealed, nor will it likely be revealed - this whale was a known troubled creature.

Is it right to keep these whales captive, so as to perform tricks for the masses of ignorant folks? Is it ethical to have people working with a whale that has had previous deaths associated to it?

The way the media presents such a circumstance is truly a deception. First, they don't reveal the footage available, because it is more than what an audience can tolerate, according to them.

Second, sensible questions that I have asked will never be asked. But to be sure, after a ceremony honoring the departed, the show went on. Sure the trainers weren't in the water with the whales for the re-opening, that would tempt the easiest of perilous nitwittery, but the whale remains and the crowds come. Even while the representation will not examine a need to avoid such another inevitable tragedy... the media, well they just keep asking questions leading the ignorant masses to heart strung emotions that mean nothing. And if they can, they exploit the future of that whale depending on what Animal Protection groups will demand. The circus and folly of Hypocronance goes on without prohibition.

There is another thing to consider for such a circumstance. If an individual feels as though maintaining captive animals is wrong, do they in fact live by their principle, or do they throw in supporting what they oppose by bringing their brood of aspiring nitwits to see the Killer Whales at Busch Gardens? If you do think it is wrong, do you still support it? The profiteers for enslaving these creatures hope you are wishy-washy on principle. That is their revenue stream. They claim to care for the creatures indentured to a tank for the purposes of enlightening the public, but you can be certain that if people didn't come to the park to see the novelty of nature as they present it that whale would be sold to some cannery paying the highest price. Likely the Japanese would make the bid securing the doom of the whale. Imagined Utopia cares very little for the constraints of the freedom and fairness it portends. Imagined Utopia must by its own nature steal from somewhere to fund the emotional need of its design.

Any economist will tell you, there is no such thing as a free lunch.

I understand that until now I have given examples of the wrongs within the folly of Hypocronance. Maybe they aren't wrongs, maybe they are just observations. The plague of Hypocronance exists because of a miserable condition of leadership. That leadership starts at the top and trickles down. It trickles down because of an example, which condones similar lacking while demonstrates a similar groove to individual leadership. Why would someone make their own journey more difficult when those above are taking the easy road? They wouldn't. Humanity rarely provides leaders capable of giving us reason to do more than we want or have to do.

You may be one of those experts in your own specificity, but you are also ignorant in the cherry picked news presented to you by an exploitive media. You may even be one who wants a better way, without actually having to commit to the steps needed to move you towards better. Politicians play the whore of media to sell you on what sounds good but truly has no realistic potential as a reality.

What I wish to do here is give you some thinking on what is needed to disperse Hypocronance as the plague it is. These next words are bits and pieces of the other piece I wrote called *The Gathering*.

The participation in learning is why we are here. True leaders accept accountability, good leaders share accountability and satisfactory leaders pass it along. If you come to learn one thing about leadership, understand leadership and accountability.

Qualifying a leader can be disposed of by seeing how a leader manages accountability. This is a natural principle. It can't be argued, it is like rain falling with a cold front passing through. Excellent leaders will always accept accountability. Here is the reason; excellent leaders avoid making poor decisions, or even selfish decisions. And even if presumed wrong, these decisions are made by policy or guidelines. There is very little room for criticism, even if the outcome of the decision was less than desirable.

Some in our country today might say that Obama and those in congress are good leaders. That is fine. They can drink their own favorite flavor of Kool-Aide. But if the words above make sense concerning leadership and accountability, how can a conclusion be made about the current leaders, when accountability for the reality has never been assumed? The current leadership in our country will not accept the role of leadership unless it is convenient for them to do so. As in the case of the Killer Whale tragedy, who in that corporation has taken accountability for the death of an employee?

In terms of our representation all I have heard is that the current administration inherited the poor conditions from the previous eight years. This on its face is an outright lie.

The majority of congress was in fact held by the opposition to the previous administration and they won't own up to the fact that their collective thinking bankrupted the financial world. Moreover, thinking about the corporation who bought the Killer Whale with two previous episodes of death resulting; I wonder if they are willing to say that the judgment to do so was probably not wise.

Excellent leadership can't be bought, unfortunately the way our political process is right now those who are elected to serve us are bought by lobbyist money. They have crafted words to suggest that campaign contributions are protected under the First Amendment and thereby legitimate for contributing to those in representation already bought by influence-pedaling corporate concerns.

While those in representation utilize the media as the whore it is, those of us with a voice are never heard unless we come en masse like in the tea party movement of late. Every talking head realizes that such a body can cripple their own function in controlling what is dispersed by need of grievance.

To this day even the media that is apparently honest can only suggest that the tea party folks are an unorganized mob with no real message. And while they report such opinions they cotton to the priority of a less than satisfactory leadership within representation. The media makes a chosen priority of Utopia's need the primary information dispersed. Just as the media will front the Utopian need of a priority of nitwittery they will also make the Utopian priority the conversation of the day and that would be due to an event of an upcoming election.

The media and those in representation are experts at spin. And as excellent leadership is always accountable, spin is never used when excellent leadership is being followed.

Now you may say none of what I have written matters, and from your perspective that may be true. My rebuttal is simply a lesson in history. If you are stuck on stupid and you listen to what the elected officials are saying without any historical reference to what they utter by the day… then you are one of the ignorant. If you accept the democrat version that the previous eight years of Bush are why we are where we are at, then you haven't been honest about the result of the '06 mid term elections.

Under President Bush, the budget was doubled, or almost doubled. Growth was typically 3-3.5%, unemployment was almost 5% consistently and the general treasury reported unexpected revenues to the tune of $50 billion a quarter for six years.

Then the democrats took the house majority, based largely on media driven antagonism against President Bush, making him a magnet for hatred. Once control of the house was taken by those of the democrat party the planning of Utopia began. All of the economic indications of a thriving economy went opposite of what they were. So by the end of his second term, the economy was in the tank and conveniently because of a majority shift in congress. The economy had paid the price for the nitwittery of progressive design.

Once times had been turned bad for the dismal leadership in congress folks were sick of the wars, sick of losing jobs, sick of corporations making more than what seemed fair and the stage was set for people to be led off the cliff of chaotic thinking, elevated to the aspirations of heartfelt comfort, by all the bullshit being spewed and spun concocted by those demanding Utopia.

Now you might think that I am a favor of Bush, but I am not. I am honest enough to say that for having a satisfactory leadership within the Bush years there were laws he signed that should have never made it out of committee. The No Child Left Behind law that he signed, which was co-authored by none other than Ted Kennedy, was the biggest bi-partisan mess ever designed.

It launched authority of educating our children from the auspices of a federal guideline which had no business dictating what should have remained as a states right issue.

Moreover, once the WMD that we went to war for was dismissed... the troops should have been deployed home. But as President Bush wanted to be a compassionate conservative, nation building was the order of business.

Thanks to the media, America was front and center for the job because the media sees globalization as a greater market share of ratings.

I thought it to be extremely funny that a private individual put President Bush up on a billboard asking, "Do ya miss me yet?" The timing of that message was not only appropriate but long overdue.

Those wanting to establish Utopia went the way of Air America and realized that without the cooperation of risk takers all they could do was battle for a losing proposition known as healthcare. And today, even if some form of it passes, it will remain a failure as it was conceived. When I heard that the notion of Universal Healthcare was a priority of this new administration all I could do was shake my head; Hilary Clinton was the last dope to try to get that done. How well did she do?

President Obama addressed both houses of congress and said that illegal aliens wouldn't be covered under his plan for healthcare. A lone congressman called him a liar. The congress was appalled. Why were they appalled?

The truth of the matter is that anyone going to an emergency room can't be asked if they are illegally here. That is a provision under the Hipaa laws congress sent to the president to sign into law.

If you are among the ignorant, knowing the correctness of the accusation you would be not appalled. However, if you were one wishing for Utopian equality, the blurting of accusation could be nothing but a lie.

The congressman later was asked for an apology for making his statement. The only thing he was wrong about was in asking for pardon. By his asking for pardon he fell from satisfactory leadership to unsatisfactory leadership and he should lose his job.

You see, folks, those who are in the business of leadership wouldn't make a claim if it were untrue, provided they were excellent leaders. They would be accountable to the fact of the matter. Unfortunately those in the media turned a blind eye to facts as they needed to be revealed and President Obama's less than unsatisfactory leadership skill was condoned.

All the while it was easier to believe that because President Obama represented altruism as presented, only the mean profit driven corrupt GOP was up to its old tricks, and you swallowed that pill all while Utopian management oversaw the greatest amount of job loss in decades. Here is the real bullet of this Utopian nonsense.

After some of the original stimulus/bailout had been spent economist's praised growth that wasn't really private growth. It was artificial growth funded by the largest grab of private wealth by the federal government.

The money realized as being a leading indicator by Utopian nitwittery was nothing more than the transfer of funds from government to businesses receiving the funds the government grabbed. And yet those of the heart strung thinking bought it up as progress towards an end of recession and/ or depression.

Even worse, many of you still think that the national unemployment rate is just under 10%. That in itself is a false number as those not receiving benefits for unemployment aren't measured.

This is to say, that if your benefit expires or depletes, you are no longer part of the measured unemployed. The hard reality of that is unknown, but I can tell you those en masse at the tea party protests reportedly came from areas where unemployment was as high as 40%.

Whether or not you accept the reality I have presented matters very little, furthermore I don't care. Even still there is a reason that the department of labor won't attempt to collect information on the unemployment rate and that reason is one they will never mention.

They may say it would be impossible to keep track of such a number, because it is beyond their capability. They would tell you that they would need a larger budget to facilitate such an undertaking and most would believe it. But the truth is they could easily satisfy the need to keep track of who was unemployed by a simple adjustment to their survey of application for benefits.

The reason why they can't be honest about such a rate is because it isn't politically beneficial to reveal the hard and brutal truth of bad times. Leadership which isn't excellent can't allow for truth to be dispersed. It won't be accountable to the reality of a condition it finds itself not being able to manage.

"I do solemnly swear that I will faithfully execute the office of President of the United States, and will to the best of my ability, protect, preserve and defend the Constitution of The United States."

Does this look familiar? It should, it is the oath of office every President takes at inauguration. Now I put these words here because the foundation of leadership is built on a foundation of power, integrity and motivation.

Obviously power is wielded by the President based upon the executive function written within the Constitution. Little needs to be said about it at this point. Motivation and Integrity are the two sides of executive power that are at the basis of why departments report data as imagined fact.

George Bush came into office largely because of who his father is, along with the power he manipulated. The man wanted a dynasty and he saw to his want. Regardless of his want and desire, his motivation brought the public to a decision resulting in Bush being elected to office.

It doesn't matter whether you liked it or not, this isn't praise for the man it is simply an example. Georgie Boy came from a conservative heritage. By his actions as President, I think it would be impossible for any conservatives to associate themselves to him.

He was a party boy with a guiding hand keeping him on the path to public service future. After Bush took the oath his actions came from consulting with those who know how to manage money and build a strong economy. That is what conservative minded people do and they do it well.

The first thing George Bush fought for, before the attacks on this country was to implement tax cuts, giving risk takers the ability to take risks in opportunity, which resulted in expansion calling for high rates of employment.

The Constitution was designed by the aristocracy leaving England to make a new world. This world was to become a place where government couldn't violate an individual's ability to life, liberty and the pursuit of happiness.

Why does George Bush's desire to cut taxes apply to the notion written in the government to protect the individual's right to life, liberty and the pursuit of happiness? Because the ability to earn money and provide a desired living Americans want is·fundamentally based upon the ability to earn money. Unless you are a communist or something other than a capitalist, that is an inarguable truth.

"I do solemnly swear that I will faithfully execute the office of President of the United States, and will to the best of my ability, protect, preserve and defend the Constitution of The United States."

Before we were attacked the simple action of cutting taxes would have been enough for President Bush to develop a comfortable legacy in terms of fulfilling his oath. The attacks happened and the entire legislative body gave authority to President Bush to do whatever he deemed necessary regarding the trouble we faced.

The action of the legislative body was a complete walk-away from the Constitutional provisions of responsible leadership within their own right as legislators.

It was in fact deplorable leadership on their behalf. Furthermore, the same representation that authorized the unilateral aggression we as a country brought to our perceived enemy all voted to fund the continued aggression.   They became hypocritical as they condemned the same aggression they approved and funded as an illegal action or as an unjust war.

They did this as a premeditated response for their loss in the 2000 general elections that swung upon the electorate in Florida. It was retaliation and the heart strung media types ran with it, thusly the tax cuts, which promised President Bush an overall approval became second to the wars we were fighting.

They saw opportunity to gain the executive office back for the following general election. The opposition's motivation was clear while their integrity as scumbag politicians was demonstrated.

Even still, with an approval by both houses to prosecute war, the President fulfilled his protection of the Constitution as we recognize a foreign threat.

Those promoting the heart strung followers of war as forever and always wrong, contrived bringing a sitting senator named John Kerry to the candidacy of the general election. They based the decision upon his winter soldier testimony, which condemned a past war, while associating his previous torments to the present war we are fighting. It wasn't a half bad idea and the nitwits of those wanting to build Utopia almost pulled it off.

The trouble was Kerry was an even bigger moron than Bush, and for the campaigning the ugliness utilized by the previous Bush campaign ensued, and the playboy Kerry was defined by his own past and perceived lack of integrity. The high paid folks seeking Utopian promise fell short of the mark because of their own hubris. We again had the second term of Bush.

The economy remained resilient and strong right up until the mid term elections I have already discussed. The only option left for the opposition was to bank on the whores within media to make the wars they still approved funding, George Bush's millstone, and that was pulled off effectively because the media influenced the ignorant masses.

It was nothing more than a Bazooka Joe chewing gum wrapper trick. Even for protecting our citizens from an enemy, which was unseen and unknown, the media vilified Bush, stating that the Patriot Act was a violation of the Constitution, even when it wasn't.

Because congress never declared war, they had another trump. In war the president can suspend any Constitutional right that he sees fit to suspend. It has been done several times in our past and it has always been legal. The contrivance of congress gave Bush authority to prosecute the war leaving them blameless as they all wanted the ignorant to believe.

When they abdicated their legislative imperative, they ensured that any leadership to come would have to rise from an extremely weakened condition, thereby making any hope for excellent leadership to follow a real problem.

This history is critical in seeing how taking the oath as President is important in determining effective leadership because the President is ultimately responsible for life, liberty and the pursuit of happiness afforded to all Americans.

For six years the facts of prosperity couldn't be argued. This country was explosive in any description of economic boon. Then the reign of conservative leadership ended in the legislative body and those demanding Utopia were literally in control and they were funded by the reality driven pimps of the media, who bashed the country and its direction to no end.

The fifth column of leftism reached the pinnacle of its desires. And what we have now defers to those wanting Utopia at any price.

President Obama was elected President without any credibility of experience for the office he was ascending towards. His unfinished term as senator for the candidacy of President demonstrated just how ignorant folks were of whom and what he was, but the majority of the ignorant felt good about the choice.

Hope and Promise were once again used in the scheme and theme of a general election and it paid off. The media had completely abdicated its authority to reveal who the candidate Obama was and they used viscous vitriol as a weapon to all those of a minority not fooled by the nitwittery.

Many of us knew that Obama wanted to grant more authority to the government in a Constitutional manner as he felt individuals couldn't be trusted to their own destiny.

The constant flow of propaganda diminished the greatness of America. Many of those who were ignorant fell for the pitch, hook line and sinker.

The charade of increasing moral value was imbued by a former vice president. His theft of an idea promoted by scientists studying the climate was the proverbial calling from a soap box, the base of want to be do-gooders known as crisis fomenting environmental stewards longed to hear.

You know the guy; he gave up on the idea that he created the Internet. Yep, Al Bore Gore. The only other guy I know as good at hood-winkin' the generally ignorant public as this guy was none other than Michael Moore.

These two dopes rallied the nitwittery in not only our country but around the world to focus about things they couldn't possibly control, but could exploit and those things are natural laws.

Some in this world can't understand balance of systems. They do however point to results of a condition with declaration of intent that it must be of a causal nature, when in fact what they point to is nothing more than a symptom.

As we have seen in the passing of time since Al Gore demanded that we were killing our world; the result was global warming. His position has been weakened by observation and admittance to wrongly concluded and wrongly figured evidence. But for the time he created an industry that rang the hungry dinner bell long waited on and they came running.

Millions were invested in an imagined industry and Obama promised in his campaign that his ten year plan to remove foreign dependence on oil made it a regular bonanza of barbecues.

Those folks who went to eat are still waitin' to digest the fruits of investment and remain drunk with remorse for following the signs to a party in need of Viagra.

All while the fool Al Bore Gore was leaving his gigantic carbon ass print on the world for traveling in his private jet and warming his 30,000 sq. ft house.

The other graduate from the PT Barnum School of thinking suggesting that there is a sucker born every minute, shook down the evil corporate enterprises that funded the same whores of media he cashed paychecks from.

Michael Moore is likely the biggest con artist ever standing next to Al Bore Gore. Both of these individuals went to war against American Institutions, not for any morally guided design.

They went to war against the institutions of America because it made them insanely wealthy as well as briefly influential amidst the fickle whores of media.

I do have to give Moore credit because of his abilities. His depictions of documentary were very close to accurate. The trouble was the depictions revealed the truth of those demanding Utopia, while they created chaos.

"A Shooting at Columbine."

Those responsible for raising the two murderous results of feel-good living allowed the school to become the killing field of indifference. And his work gave the revelation, a conversation that immediately became a priority so schools could become aware of the ineptitude they previously managed.

So while the ignorant masses spent their money in unorganized fashion to believe in change that was represented by the words Yes We Can,

America ushered in a President who has done what he thought was a version of the oath of office, one which had to be restated for absolute correctness of misspeak.

If you can still read what I have written, if it isn't offensive to your sensibilities, you should now understand what the plague of Hypocronance yields. Hypocronance is the combining of hypocrisy and ignorance sold by an institution uninterested in anything other than rating share or profit. The same profit by the two shakedown artists mentioned above. And these aren't the only two, nor are they from only one side of the political spectrum.

Politicians by definition use cunning and trickery to persuade the masses of ignorance. Now I am not going to say all politicians are politicians because that just isn't the case. In the realm of politicians there are those who go as public servants.

In the face of the most impossible temptations to sell out, some stay to the core of serving the public. Unless you are a student of the political circus and unless you have the wisdom to listen between the words of the abdicated doctrines of former journalism within the media, it is likely that you may not know the difference of politician to public servant.

Maybe you just don't want to know and that is more than I can care about because the only thing I hate in this world is abject stupidity.

So if you are of a one-sided mind and think that somehow those who want and demand government regulated Utopia or a more fair and kind world, then I really have no use for you.

The disregard those of you give to individualism as being our greatest national asset is very troubling to me.

You see, those who don't follow critical thinking aren't in the business of employing folks. Many of these thinkers never have employed folks, but they are sure ready to cast an envious eye on those willing to risk everything once they hit pay dirt.

Those of you who don't understand that compensation of a privately negotiated contract is not your business, I say to you - mind your own business! CEOs who run the evil corporations that produce goods, which you buy to live in luxury do negotiate their own compensation because of their abilities as corporate executive officers.

If you think they need to pay a fair share required to run your Utopia it proves only one thing. You are ignorant of taxation in this country or you are just stupid with envy. If you were honest about your envy or your stupidity you would install public servants into government who would bring the business of change to the debate floor within the houses of congress. That would be the only honorable way to dispose of your envy, and then let it stand the test of willingness by majority vote to become new law.

In the design of Utopia and a more fair and kind type of a world, you would have to demonstrate a moral imperative to change the system as it is currently designed. Moreover, if you weren't ignorant you'd realize that demanding taxation by representation is a Constitutional certainty, which has been over-ridden by the established representation we already have.

The Fed and the Electoral College vote were after the fact amendments to the Constitution. In fact our representation has been diminished by the very words within the Constitution as an original document.

There was to be one congressman per every 30,000 citizens of a voting district. Why do you think that was changed? Do you even have a clue? It was changed because those in the business of representation didn't want to manage the consensus needed to pass legislation as directed by the original drafting of the Constitution. In other words... politicians and lobbyists wanted to minimize control of the legislative process.

Moreover, they wanted to by design of the FED manipulate your personal holding of wealth to avoid catastrophe they themselves brought to us for their own ineptitude.

This is all ancient process of law and likely very few of you understand it, but not understanding it doesn't make it invalid. It just proves even more that many of you are ignorant of the evolution of our system.

I don't want anyone to feel as though because you are ignorant I am slighting you.

That isn't the intention of this piece. The intention of this piece is for your enlightenment, rather than just an undirected and unfocused ridicule of what you are. Progressivism and the thinking of progressivism is older than most of you.

The ideals in progressivism gave power to men and women and children during times when big business operated with great unethical standards. Unions and the development of organized labor were the original motivations for such collective thinking.

The organizing of workers, men, women and children's life standards benefited. So at the outset unionizing was apparently a very good thing. The trouble unionizing came to was the same bureaucratic nightmare that the representation of the land had, otherwise known as greed.

Greed of power, greed of wealth, greed of influence became the negotiation of all organizing labor influences that brought innovations to the world. The very same greed was harnessed in overcoming modern day tyranny in old Europe, by naming it patriotism.

This is another natural law men face in dealing with the value of material. It can be said that losing a contract in a bid for business is similar to losing a fight for engaging an enemy. The loser goes home empty handed and sometimes faces loss of the job or of the country for the respective battle it faces. The natural truth here is the quality of life is redeemed for earning money. It takes money to make a business presentation as does it take money to fight a war. The award for success in either battle or business is freedom to control your destiny.

Through the progressive movement business realized that they would have to share wealth because for sharing the wealth it could still make a nice and comfortable profit. But the more progressivism grew, the fatter the public became all while enjoying more leisure time, which made available for less production and greater benefit to the employed.

The other side of that equation is another natural law known as less profit. Once a margin of profit can no longer be realized, those creating the atmosphere of profitability tend to look for more profit elsewhere.

If you don't believe that as a truth then you are plainly stupid. You see you may feel entitled to be guaranteed a good salary or good benefits for working, but that is all based upon the gain of the risk takers. Once your cost as an employee becomes prohibitive to the risk taker's ability to make a profit, you become expendable as a liability. This is nothing more than a mathematical equation any person seeking gain applies to a condition. They ask themselves if the risk that they are considering is worth a chance of gain. That is as simple as it gets.

Because progressivism gained influence and authority, many of our younger citizens rarely knew hardship, and with the benefit of education and potential to be decision makers in profitability's motivation the margin of profitability grew to be less and less. It became obvious that the business of employing those who felt entitled to rewards built from their ancestry's efforts became more trouble than they were worth.

Governance also helped along this reality by creating a safety net for the people it represented. Governance always cost the same profit risk takers had to divvy between two different liabilities.

Business was faced with the liability associated to paying labor and a growing regulatory authority granted to a government that already manipulated the Constitution for its own minimizing of power.

Today, because of labor unionizing and entitlement of a less motivated work force the unsustainable costs for doing business have driven those seeking profit away from our culture.

Media, government and ignorance of the masses are available to blame the risk takers of our country as evil and greedy, without morality. This is because of their own excesses of gain as unsustainable earnings for overpaid jobs they have, forgot that the margin of profit is what delivered them to their own quality of life.

So the reality is their own greed as employees priced them right out of their own jobs. Representation of the same employee based citizenry along with a media lacking integrity make up the envious result of progressive intention. Meaning, they desired and demanded a more fair and kind of Utopia now trying to be manipulated by the current leadership of representation.

The only manner in which this could be accomplished was to hoodwink a primed percentage of the populace into thinking that they as the YES WE CAN crowd could do better than going along on a desired path, without the benefit of those able to assume risk. And those folks today are known as lenders.

Today after years of promises stated without any intention of fulfillment, let alone a plan to accomplish them; we are faced with those in leadership who will do nothing more than blame the past leadership for their ineffectiveness all while demanding a false Utopia of moral imperative based upon a false right never attributed in our founding document, known as Healthcare.

Forget the promises of redeploying troops, or working towards a business ensuring our ability to get out from under our dependence on foreign oil because they aren't going to happen. You see that was all smoke and mirrors displayed to take control of a system the ignorant believe as a right, otherwise known as Universal Healthcare. Don't believe me?

Ya don't have to, but you will want to examine who the greatest employer in the near future is going to be. Why is that the case? Well it goes back to the avoiding reality that all life is born to die.

It goes back to thinking health defects really aren't nature's way of population control. It feeds the notion that all life is sacred and should be protected even when the proposition of protecting life is ridiculous.

Once again those who control how healthcare gets managed in this country are going to be in a position of power, based upon a Utopia the ignorant masses feel entitled to, hoping for a Utopia of healthy and long lived life based upon a notion that it is a right instead of a personal obligation.

Just as life isn't fair, neither is the certainty that your genetic make-up isn't problem free. Many are born by people who weren't meant to live more than a certain amount of years. Without the reason of science or the benefit of research most people usually died off before 61. As a matter of fact the age the social security actuaries worked on as a given was a life expectancy of 61.

The insurance policy then was rigged to provide benefits after retirement for about a year, all while the government demanded a tax on every employee matched by the employer to pay for the insurance program they designed. See, once again it is proven laws of nature can't be argued.

The government in the early days of Social Security came into a windfall of revenue promoted by the notion of a Utopian society whereas government began taking care of the citizen from cradle to grave, which was purely a result of progressive thinking and implementation of policy. What those geniuses didn't look to was the unexpected result that those they insured wouldn't die within the 1-5 year plan they made assumptions on.

After realizing more benefit could be controlled for extended living of workers. Those responsible for managing profit earnings and taxable revenue created a treasure chest the government could fudge. Then they learned how to legislate all other kinds of really cool and useless laws we now have in place today within the context of a better quality of living. The trouble with this is the government never realized the revenue generated by those working would come to an end as the Baby Boomers came off of high tax rates for being well compensated through employment and went onto the system they had funded, now as liabilities.

Maybe the thinking was that new workers would fund the bill and even if they determined an increase in taxation needed to be written into law. The government proceeded with arrogance, not paying attention to future prospects. Guess what... for the last 20 years of my adult life I have seen four times when the Social Security question has been bantered as problematic and going broke. Why? Well, fewer workers mean less contribution to a greater capacity needing payouts never expected in the original design of the system.

As I learned it in my days of college, the inception of Social Security benefits had 16 contributors to one payee. The reality of today is almost exactly the inverse. Now I ask you, if you have one contributor to 16 payouts what do you get? Thankfully those wanting Utopia have designed a greater capacity to tax employees and non employees to make up the difference all while they say it is in the general welfare of it citizenry. Not only do they get an income tax, they get a sales tax, they get a property tax, they get a death tax, they get an earned interest tax. If you follow all the taxes you have to pay to the last dollar you'd find that for every dollar you make you are paying at least 50% to taxes in summation of earning every one dollar. And then of course we have those folks who get an income for nothing but living, even if it is in our own worst interest to support them.

That, my friends, goes straight back to the heart strung feeling of managing our resources. Hypocronance is everyone's condition just as dying is the truth of reality. When we speak of death, we speak of abhorrence to something we know to be true. We think of it as the end of living and it is unsettling. At least for those of us who aren't aware that we are born to die.

What I am going to present is nothing that the nitwittery of the ignorant will tolerate. As a matter of fact once I publish this work, I am going to apply for a permit to carry a gun because what I am telling you is the truth, which will give you reason to hate me.

I say this because of the differences people see according to their own morality for living. Remember, morality is an individual's terms of reckoning that which is wrong or right. Some folks think that those born to this world are innocent and do so because of their faith.

I can tell you that no person born is innocent. Every person born comes to this world with all the intentions and choices God provided. However those born to children, have very little choice. Now some think abortion for birth control is a sin.

I say again just as we are not born innocent it is because we were born to sin. We are imperfect. However, for myself I am perfectly imperfect. That is reckoned by my faith and none of you need believe what I say.

The point of this conversation is the understanding of how we come to see our purpose. If you are of the mind that there is no definitional difference of killing and murder, then you are a heart strung person believing that Utopia can exist. And for that belief you promote a demonstration of Hypocronance better than any example I have previously outlined.

Some of you may oppose the death penalty, some may say the death penalty is wrong and if you are of that ilk, I say you are a consummate nitwit. Killing is condoned whether or not you wish to believe it. Self preservation is the sum of life, liberty and the pursuit of happiness, even if you only read picture books.

If someone is bringing death to you it is intentional and therefore murder. If in the face of a murderous thug, you manage to kill the offender, you do so by the rights guaranteed to us by our Creator. Even as stupid as man's designs are or may be, everyone has a right to self defense. That being mentioned; it makes killing and murder two very different things. Why is the distinction important? Well, because it is the foundation upon other ways to look at the ending of life.

Let us examine a medical procedure known as abortion... If you are of the mind that abortion is wrong, I have no problem with that thinking, unless of course you are unwilling to deal with the result of not having abortion as a medical procedure. Once you determine a child should live because his parents abdicated the responsibility of being parents, much like the media did with journalistic integrity, what happens for the result? Will you be willing to raise the child to become an independent citizen or are you ready to allow the hellish nightmare of a bureaucratic curse to raise that child?

If you are supportive of the above because of your heart strung Utopianism, I would suggest that you make provisions to raise the child within the framework on which governance can be addressed. That ultimately means that the child will be raised as a monster, you'll all deal with the condition because you provided the life without rearing them. This is to say that you saved the child's life counting on the fact that government would raise them as you would raise your own. And even if that was true, how good of a parent are you?

Here is the point. We have those who are known to be repetitive violators of human sanctity who live because you don't know the definition of murder and killing.

We have those who you think are born innocently, and maybe they are, but they are without responsible raising and only become individuals without knowing how to be independent. They ultimately end up being a liability to our society.

Both thoughts are weak and heart strung emotive notions, which only make our condition more burdened. Why? Because those of you who think healthcare is a responsibility owned by any other than he or she responsible for their own health is your folly of Hypocronance.

That is the hubris and prideful thinking of those who never understood how to make a payroll. All while they expected a certainty of having a job, which would enable their envious nature to live while allowing that which should be put down for one logical reason or another.

Logic dictates you either cure a problem or you kill the problem. If in fact you can't cure recitative behavior, do you fund it? If you save a life that has no hope to be independent will you support it? These questions are what conservative people ask when they contemplate leadership because they know there is a budget to living peacefully and in good quality.

Those of you who think life should be fair or beyond reproach of sin have heart felt emotive responses to either the exactness of curing or killing a problem before the problem becomes critical in nature. Here is the worst part; the progressives and the evil born again worshippers of deity are on opposite sides of their own congruity.

Both sides argue against the sanctity of life and it is likely none of them welcome the notion that we are all born to die. Even worse are the profiteers who will deny the logic concerning sanctity in life, liberty and the pursuit of happiness as it was once known in our heritage.

More to that fact is the quasi-governmental agencies oversight of both penal and foster care agencies, which demand funding by the public of ignorant masses who cannot or will not face as singular truth to living peacefully.

That truth would equal to a notion that there is a difference to killing and murder. While murder is a truth we all have to deal with directly or indirectly, killing is something we'd avoid with passion for the sake of our own brand of Utopianism.

How is it that incurable sex offenders return to a public while we know that they will offend again? If it walks like a duck, and it sounds like a duck, and swims like a duck… is it not a duck? Why do we invite a certainty of violation against our own best interest again and again? Why do we save the life of an innocent to only insure that they become victim to non loving environs we all want for the sake of our thinking while we consider righteousness as something we claim as a deity, without knowing faith?

Why do we burden ourselves with a cure that doesn't exist? Because each and every one of us buy insurance to give our families what we didn't give to them while we were here, otherwise known as an ability to live as rugged individuals responsible to our own condition. And guess who is in the middle of that nightmare.

Those of representation and the media, both of them take huge revenues to insure that you remain ignorant. Here is the real bitch; you fund it all. You pay the taxes, you watch the shows, you live your life, and if you aren't payin' attention you become owned by the future; full of fearing of the inevitable and wanting to delay your ineptly prepared legacy; wishing for a bailout.

Here ya go folks, the whole point of your need… the aspiration to your existence, the inalienable right, granted to you by your Creator, bound by man's law… Life, Liberty and the Pursuit of Happiness…

What is your Happiness? What is your risk of gain? Do you stand in your own morality? Individuals gathering would have a tough time answering the three questions to like-mindedness of being similar to the asking.

Is it easier to be the fainting witness of the coming of a new Messiah? Or is it easier to be called a racist for disagreeing with people who demand Utopia?

I don't want to mention this was all happening while everyone was buying what they'd come to regret the purchase for later. I posted as much.

One year ago, you couldn't not feel support for Obama... well I felt it, as ridiculous as it was to feel such a way. Through it all I was a skeptic, I heard what he said and told those I knew he was a ringer. Some loved him, and some hated him. Others where imbued by the mania. Some were discontented with the whole process, they just didn't care... they gave up.

There was the minority who asked, "What the fuck is wrong with this picture?" None of us who asked are surprised at all that occurred, in fact we told folks it won't matter because the pain coming had no end.

We were called racists... whatever else you can imagine for seeing the truth as it was presented. Some remained silent to talk about it, some condemned me for what I was speaking to as a seer. Yet here we contemplate our own Hypocronance, if you can even understand what the word means?!

The general welfare of a country isn't the obligation of seeking a Utopia. The general welfare of this country is to see to the inalienable rights of individuals so they can determine their own freedom based upon their own choice of a higher power. If that higher power be man's choice to figure, then you'd be good as a scientist of some sort, making the quantity of man's capability well known and defined. Similarly, if you knew your Creator as a motivation of gain to your own condition, you might end up as a risk taker, and if you knew your higher power through intolerable suffering you might feel cursed.

The purpose of government isn't a folly of a dynamic conjured by three faces of ineptitude, proclaiming an authority granted to others for their own negligence. The purpose of the American government is to promote a general welfare of its people abiding that everyone has a choice to fulfill their own destiny as they see fit collectively interested in their own condition as individuals. Americans aren't the type to step aside for such an invasion.

Unless of course you thought the purpose of government was to insure your own general welfare, which is born in the nature of progressive thinking; making you accountable to nothing of your own design, but dependent on the favor of who you can get to say, "Yes, We Can" more convincingly than you can. All while you deny the reality that allowing the centralized folly of Hypocronance to spread...

You claim I lie?

Take a look at the Obama projected budget and tell me faced with our cultural issues we can afford his billions going to places that know nothing of American Bravery and Courage!

Dare ya. Ya CAN"T

Those of you who think Yes We Can works... let me ask ya two questions. Do you think we can afford Obama's billions going to the rest of the world, while we give up our own destiny to be more then the result of a folly of Hypocronance, or do we take it upon ourselves to make our own welfare our own interest, rather than leave it up to a governing body uninterested in representing us, while they claim to be interested in our welfare, while they sell us to an idea of Utopia, contradicting the American reality which is the envy of the world.
Completely envisioned by a medium that abdicated the same authority for their purpose of being, while the ignorant gave up a studied and logically reasoned thought giving us an ability to see to our own welfare?

How the hell did the ignorant rise to elect President Obama? How did they see to elect President Obama after the result of the 2006 elections? Can you say Chaos?

Look... all of us have an ability to shine as individuals and in that shine we seek to be human. Humanity is an enduring race if not proficient at overcoming limitations of natural laws. But we don't only overcome natural laws... we create scenarios that give us reason to forget our own needs. My friends... if you ever wondered why we have unhappiness in a land on the globe as so bountiful and free as we exist, it is because of a document written by those braver then we could ever imagine to be. They walked away from everything they knew as a provider of a general welfare managed by something other than a group depending on the folly of Hypocronance. That group of people is sold to us by the addiction of our boredom and you can call it our media and representation and our own ignorance....

In this country, *We the People* get what we allow or demand...

How is that Obama vote workin' out for you?

Or better yet, how is that progressive vote makin' your quality of life?

The hope of this world isn't found in demanding Utopia, hope is known by embracing the inalienable rights granted to us by our Creator defined by the laws of men, known as life, liberty and pursuit of happiness. Life enlightened is living simply as free men and women existing perfectly as imperfect, knowing that life is a gift and that we are born to die.

FIN

Martin H. Petry is the author of The Hard Justice Series, including The Violation, Peregrination, Expurgation and Final Destination. He is currently working on the fifth book in the series; Terminus. He has also written two books of poetry; By the Eyes of a Poet and Facing a Mirror. Venturing into the realm of non-fiction he's penned The Curtailed Tails of Mutt Justify, a collection of three short stories, and has co-authored Convoking Hell and Conjuring Love with his editor, Tracy LeCates. All his works are available on USAMutt.com

★★★★★ *Hard Justice: The Violation*, December 2, 2009
Surreal and enlightening with cutting-edge spy gadgetry, I found this book to be heart wrenching with a touch of wit and humor that brings it alive and captivates you to read on... striving to find justice in an unjust world.

★★★★★ *Peregrination excellent sequel*, August 17, 2009
"Peregrination" follows the characters and situations created in "The Violation" very well and builds on the story logically and beautifully! I also purchased the third book in the series and am starting it with enthusiasm.

★★★★★ **Convoking Hell An amazingly bold, honest, and masterfully woven life account of pain, survival, hope, and love..**, *December 4, 2009*
Convoking Hell is a brutally honest tale in which the authors both bare their souls. Souls tortured and tormented by the lives/bodies their beautiful spirits were placed into. Not many could have survived the pain, abuse and humiliation that these two beautiful and creative spirits endured. It is truly a page turning cannot put down book.

★★★★★ **Convoking Hell Gritty and impossible to put down!**, *November 16, 2009*
Their stories are heartbreaking and yet, bring hope to others who are struggling. And their stories show the ugly truth about what growing up in Ridgefield was like. This story of a town of such affluence, yet with such secrets, and where image was so important that no one spoke the truth about what was going on in their homes, will leave you with more questions than answers.

★★★★★ **~ By the Eyes of a Poet * Beautifully written poetry ***
Every poem seems to touch a part of your life, the seen and the unseen alike. Amazing, high five stars!! A MUST READ!!

5132755R0

Made in the USA
Lexington, KY
07 April 2010